The Beginner's Guide

Figure Drawing

A complete step–by–step guide to techniques and materials

D1122824

HILLSBORO PUBLIC LIBRARIES
Hillsboro, OR
Member of Washington County
COOPERATIVE LIBRARY SERVICES

The Beginner's Guide

Figure Drawing

A complete step–by–step guide to techniques and materials

PATRICIA MONAHAN
with
Albany Wiseman

NEW HOLLAND

HILLSBORO PUBLIC LIBRARIES
Hillsboro, OR
Member of Washington County
COOPERATIVE LIBRARY SERVICES

First published in 2000 by
New Holland Publishers (UK) Ltd
London • Cape Town • Sydney • Auckland

24 Nutford Place
London W1H 6DQ
UK

80 McKenzie Street
Cape Town 8001
South Africa

Level 1, Unit 4, 14 Aquatic Drive
Frenchs Forest, NSW 2086
Australia

Unit 1A, 218 Lake Road
Northcote, Auckland
New Zealand

10 9 8 7 6 5 4 3 2 1

Copyright © 2000 New Holland Publishers (UK) Ltd

All rights reserved. No part of this publication may be reproduced,
stored in a retrieval system, or transmitted in any form or by any means,
electronic, mechanical, photocopying, recording or otherwise,
without the prior written permission of the
publishers and copyright holders.

ISBN 1 85974 164 9 *2939 1+21 10/03*

Designed and edited by
Phoebus Editions Limited
City House, 72/80 Leather Lane
London EC1N 7TR

Editor: Patsy North
Designer: Louise Morley
Photographer: George Taylor

Reproduction by Colour Symphony in Singapore
Printed and bound in Malaysia by Times Offset (M) sdn Bhd

ACKNOWLEDGEMENTS
All step-by-step demonstrations and artworks are by Albany Wiseman unless otherwise credited.
Special thanks are due to the models who posed for the drawings in this book –
Nadia Dean, Stephen Fall, Felicitas Grabe and Sarah Hickey.

CONTENTS

INTRODUCTION 6

MATERIALS AND EQUIPMENT 10

APPROACHES TO DRAWING THE FIGURE 14

GALLERY 18

EXERCISES

 1 DRAWING IN LINE AND TONE 22

 2 DRAWING ACCURATELY 30

 3 THE MOVING FIGURE 38

 4 BONES, MUSCLE AND BALANCE 46

 5 HEADS, HANDS AND FEET 54

 6 LIGHTING THE FIGURE 62

 7 DRAWING GROUPS OF PEOPLE 70

INDEX 80

INTRODUCTION

For the artist, the human figure is infinitely absorbing and inspiring – it is a subject to which Western artists have returned time and time again. Attitudes to the human body and the way it is depicted in art have varied throughout the centuries and seem to reflect a society's social structures and religious beliefs, as well as its views on the importance of the individual. In fact, concern with the portrayal of the human form is not universal; the art of Islam prohibits the depiction of any living creature on religious grounds.

The art of ancient Egypt was a funerary art, designed to glorify a dead pharaoh or other powerful person and to magically ensure that the dead were supplied with all their needs in the afterlife. The figures in surviving tomb paintings have a flat, stylized quality, with clear, crisp outlines infilled with flat

colour. Each part of the figure was depicted from its most recognizable angle. Feet were shown from the side, one in front of the other, while the head was in profile with the eye shown from the front. The shoulders were straight on, hips and legs were in three-quarter view and the torso was slightly turned. Identity was established by inscriptions rather than physical likeness. Artists were craftsmen who worked to a rigid set of rules and Egyptian art changed little over 3,000 years.

The Ancient Greeks were concerned with the ideal beauty of gods, heroes and humans. From ancient writers we know that they attributed great importance to drawing, but the best record of Greek figurative art is their pottery which was elaborately decorated. Prior to the fifth century BC, the figuration was geometric, stylized and worked

Dancers on a Bench
Edgar Degas (1834–1917)
Pastel on tinted paper

Degas was a virtuoso draughtsman who drew from the model in a range of media. He achieved glowing flesh tones in his pastel paintings by overlaying strokes in many different colours. Despite their apparent spontaneity, his 'finished' pastels and paintings were usually made in the studio.

An Actor Standing
Rembrandt van Rijn (1606–1669)
Chalk on tinted paper

Dutch artist Rembrandt was a gifted and insightful student of the human form. In this assured drawing, he has used a variety of techniques to capture the volumes of the figure, using fine lines in the lighter areas and applying the chalk with more vigour for the darker tones and heavy creases of the actor's cloak.

black on red. Later, in the classical period, figures were picked out in red against a black ground and were elaborated with line to give the forms more detail and solidity. Artists also attempted to suggest space and recession by overlapping elements. These drawings, made 2,500 years ago, look remarkably modern and realistic.

The Life Class *Edward Ardizzone (1900–1979)*
Line and watercolour

The English artist and illustrator, Edward Ardizzone, had a marvellous ability to sum up a character with a bold, gestural outline. Cartoonists and illustrators must convey the essence of a subject quickly and efficiently, and this requires excellent draughtsmanship and knowledge of the human form.

The Romans borrowed heavily from Etruscan and Hellenistic art. They were more concerned with the actual rather than the ideal view of the figure and produced some very realistic 'warts and all' portraits.

The Renaissance was crucial to the development of Western European art and culture. It can be dated from the early fifteenth century in Florence, reaching its high point in the early sixteenth century, by which time it had spread to the rest of Europe. It was a time of intellectual and artistic upheaval and revival. Portraiture and mythological themes became popular and artists sought to represent the human figure naturalistically. They studied proportion and explored ways of depicting solid form, space and depth. This interest in anatomy can be seen in the sketchbooks of Leonardo da Vinci (1452–1519),

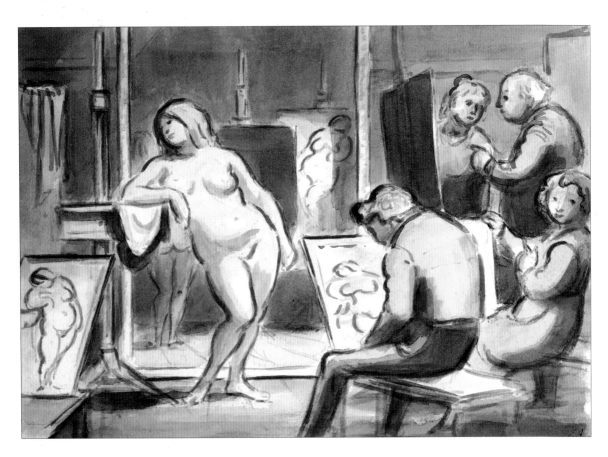

which include studies of dissections. The Renaissance was also a time of technical innovation. Artists used a range of drawing media including chalks, charcoal, pen and ink, brush and wash and silverpoint – a technique which used metal wires to create a line on a prepared support. Drawings were used as preparations for paintings, but they were also made as artworks in their own right.

By the seventeenth century, artists were drawing with greater freedom, using a flowing, expressive line. Rembrandt van Rijn (1606–1669) was a master draughtsman with a succinct but lively line. Among his many portraits, he captured the continuing concern with scientific research into the human body in his paintings *The Anatomy Lesson of Dr Tulp* (1632) and *The Anatomical Lesson of Dr Joan Deyman* (1656) in which he depicts the dissection of a human brain.

During the Rococo period in the eighteenth century, France produced brilliant draughtsmen in François Boucher (1703–1770), Jean-Honoré Fragonard (1732–1806) and Jean Antoine Watteau (1684–1721), whose drawings were lively, colourful and charming. With the classical revival at the end of the eighteenth century, free drawing and the spirit of frivolity were abandoned in favour of a more severe style epitomised by Jacques-Louis David (1748–1825) and Jean-Auguste-Dominique Ingres (1780–1867).

Later artists valued an even more personal and expressive style. Vincent van Gogh (1853–1890) used reed pen to create vigorous, often decorative images. Edgar Degas (1834–1917) drew from the model throughout his life, and sometimes recycled a composition by tracing it several times and reworking it in different colours and tones to create a series of variations on the original theme. He was a master draughtsman in many media, including pastel, often using strong, almost expressionist colour.

In the twentieth century, figure drawing has produced many exponents, from Henri Matisse (1869–1954), with his decorative use of flat colour, to Pablo Picasso (1881–1973), who could encompass a figure in a single line.

The Gleaner *Georges Seurat (1859–1891)*
Conté crayon

In this simple, evocative drawing, Seurat has built up the dark, stooping figure from layers of wispy, agitated strokes. He has set the bold image against a light sky, so that it is seen in silhouette. This emphasizes the strong shape created by the curve of the man's back and his bent limbs.

You can learn an enormous amount from the great artists of the past and the present. Their drawings of the human form offer the aspiring artist a huge, varied and inspiring resource which can be studied in galleries, museums, books and prints. By looking at the human figure through their eyes, you will see it in a new way, finding solutions to problems and discovering innovative and exciting ways of using materials.

MATERIALS AND EQUIPMENT

The medium you choose for a drawing will depend on your personal taste and the purpose of the drawing. Here we look at the most important black and grey drawing media; on pages 12 and 13, the coloured drawing media are reviewed.

GRAPHITE MEDIA

Graphite pencils are the simplest, cheapest and most flexible of all the artist's drawing tools. They are available in about 20 grades of hardness: soft pencils are designated 8B to B, with 8B the softest, while hard pencils range from H to 10H, which is the hardest. HB is medium grade.

The character of a pencil mark depends on the hardness or softness of the pencil, the degree of pressure applied, the sharpness of the drawing tip and the texture of the support used. For the best papers to use, see page 13.

Graphite sticks are available in two forms: hexagonal sticks of pure graphite and rounded sticks with a plastic sheath to keep your hands clean. They range from HB to 9B and are useful for a range of techniques including applying broad areas of tone, smudging and blending.

Graphite powder is ideal for large scale work and broad tonal effects, but it is messy to work with. The powder can be applied with your finger tips or a soft cloth, and blended with a torchon

A dip pen used with ink is a traditional drawing tool. Experiment with different nibs and with quill, reed and bamboo (right) pens. You will find that they are easy to use and wonderfully responsive.

(see opposite). It combines well with pencil or graphite sticks. Use it to create quick, gestural drawings of the moving figure.

CHARCOAL

Charcoal is an expressive medium with a velvety quality. It is made from burnt vine, willow or beech twigs and comes in a range of thicknesses. It is also available as compressed sticks and pencils, which are harder than natural charcoal. Charcoal is ideal for life studies, because its soft,

crumbly line encourages you to work boldy and broadly. It offers a combination of line and tone and is easy to erase.

CONTÉ PENCILS

Conté pencils are a type of hard pastel or chalk encased in wood to make them cleaner and more convenient to use. They make dark marks that can be smudged and blended.

PENS

Pen and ink can be used for pure line or for rendered tones using hatching, cross-hatching or stippling techniques.

Dip pens consist of a shaft into which you insert the nib of your choice. The pen is dipped into the ink and recharged from time to time.

Fountain pens have a reservoir of ink, either in the form of a replaceable cartridge or with a refillable pump-action. They are useful for sketching away from home as you don't have to carry a bottle of ink with you.

Quill pens are cut from goose feathers and have a tough, rather scratchy quality. They produce a characterful line.

Bamboo pens are chunky and pleasant to use, but are less pliant than quill pens.

Reed pens are thinner than bamboo, but have similar qualities.

INKS

Inks are either waterproof or water-soluble. Waterproof inks, such as Indian ink, dry to a non-soluble film. When a wash is laid over lines drawn in this kind of ink, they remain intact. Marks made with water-soluble inks, on the other hand, can be softened with water and blended. Waterproof inks are usually shellac-based and should only be used with dip pens or a brush – they will clog the mechanism of fountain pens.

ACCESSORIES

A craft knife is better than a pencil sharpener to sharpen pencils, as it allows you to control the shape of the tip more precisely. You can make a long, fine point for detailed work, or a blunt or wedge-shaped tip for shading. Pencil sharpeners are convenient but less flexible and sometimes cause the lead to break in the shaft. Rub a pencil on a piece of glasspaper to bring it to a sharp point, or to soften the sharpened point. You can buy small tear-off pads of glasspaper from art supply shops.

Erasers are used with all dry drawing media to make corrections, but also to pull out highlights and create textures. The most useful type of eraser is a kneadable putty rubber. Because it is soft, it won't damage the paper surface. You can can also pull off a piece and work it into a point to erase details.

Torchons, also known as stumps or tortillons, are pencil-shaped tools made of compressed or rolled paper. They have tapered or pointed ends and are used for blending pastel, pencil, charcoal or graphite.

Fixative is necessary for most dry media to prevent the drawing from smudging. It can be applied using an atomizer or a mouth-spray, and is also available in aerosol cans.

A drawing board provides a firm surface to which you can attach loose sheets of paper. Use it on an easel, on a work top or on your knee. A piece of 6mm (¼in) plywood will make a good, light board. If you are going to use it for stretching watercolour paper, you should seal both sides.

Indian ink

dip pen

charcoal sticks: thick and thin

white chalk

hexagonal graphite stick

charcoal pencil

round graphite stick

black Conté pencil

2B pencil

torchon

putty rubber

glasspaper

pencil sharpener

craft knife

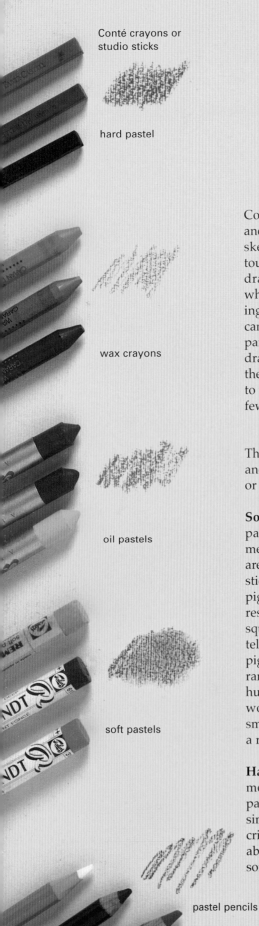

Conté crayons or studio sticks

hard pastel

wax crayons

oil pastels

soft pastels

pastel pencils

COLOURED MEDIA

Colour undoubtedly adds another dimension to even the sketchiest figure study. Tiny touches of colour will enliven a drawing or add emphasis, while a fully worked-up drawing in coloured pencil or pastel can have as much impact as a painting. There is a wealth of drawing media on the market – the problem is deciding which to use. Here, we review just a few of the products available.

DRY MEDIA

The dry media are convenient and simple to use in the studio or on location.

Soft pastels are the most painterly of all the drawing media – in fact, works in pastel are often called paintings. The sticks of pastel are made up of pigment bound with gum or resin and may be round or square in cross section. Soft pastels contain a high proportion of pigment and are available in a range of tints and tones of each hue. They can be used for line work or stippled, hatched, smudged and blended to create a range of effects.

Hard pastels are firmer and more chalk-like than soft pastels. They can be used in a similar way, but they give a crisper line and are less blendable. You can combine both sorts of pastel to good effect,

using soft pastels for broad areas of colour and adding details with hard pastels.

Pastel pencils are hard pastels in pencil form. They are cleaner to use than traditional pastels and can be sharpened to a fine point, but have a drier, more crumbly line than ordinary coloured pencils. All drawings in pastel (except oil pastel) should be fixed with a spray fixative to prevent smudging.

Oil pastels are very different from soft pastels. They consist of pigment bound with oil and wax and have a greasy texture which is similar to wax crayon. They are mostly used in combination with other media such as oil paint in mixed media work.

Wax crayons are firmer and less oily than oil pastels. They can be used for quick sketches or in mixed media studies.

Conté crayons, often called studio sticks, consist of compressed pigment with a binder. They are square in cross-section and are commonly available in a range of natural earth pigments such as umber, sanguine and ochre, as well as sepia, which is not an earth colour. Conté crayons are ideal for doing monochrome studies, especially if they are used together with a little white chalk for the highlights.

liquid acrylic

tinted papers

coloured ink

coloured pencils

fibre-tipped pens

water-soluble
coloured pencils

Coloured pencils have traditionally been hard and waxy with a crisp line. Nowadays, many ranges are much softer, and can be smudged with the finger or blended with spirit. Coloured pencils are ideal for line drawing with areas of tone and colour created by hatching and cross-hatching. As they are clean to use and easy to carry about, they are excellent for working on location.

Water-soluble pencils are becoming increasingly popular, because they are so flexible. They can be used for line work and hatching in the same way as coloured pencils, but they can also be softened and blended to a wash with water. Interesting effects can also be achieved by using them on a damp surface, or by dipping the tip of the pencil into water. Some brands are more blendable than others – it is worth experimenting to find out which suits your style.

Fibre-tipped pens are available in a wide range of transparent, vivid colours. They may be water-soluble or spirit-based, with fine, blunt or brush-like tips, and are useful for quick coloured sketches.

LIQUID MEDIA
Pens and brushes can be used for drawing with a range of liquid coloured media.

Coloured inks are transparent and have a jewel-like brilliance. Most of them are dye-based and therefore fugitive, i.e. they fade on exposure to light, so they are most suitable to use in sketchbooks, where they will be less exposed to the light.

Liquid watercolours are also dye-based and fugitive, but they dry to a soluble film, unlike the coloured inks, which are water-resistant.

Liquid acrylics are pigment-based and bound in an acrylic medium. They dry to form a permanent film and are lightfast. There are many different ranges on the market – some are transparent like traditional inks, while others are opaque.

PAPERS
Choose paper that is compatible with the medium you are using. Smooth paper is an ideal surface for work in hard graphite pencil, coloured pencil, or pen and ink, while a paper with more texture, such as Ingres paper, enhances crumbly media such as soft pastels or charcoal. Pastels work particularly well on tinted paper.

Watercolour paper provides a firm background for drawings done in water-soluble coloured pencils or for those tinted with watercolour paint. For a useful general-purpose surface, keep a good supply of cartridge paper.

APPROACHES TO DRAWING THE FIGURE

The figure is probably the most important subject in the artist's repertoire. As human beings, we have a natural interest in investigating and recording our own kind, but our close involvement with the subject can make drawing the figure seem more daunting than it really is. One of the aims of this book is to help you rid yourself of preconceptions and see the figure as an abstract assemblage of shapes, volumes, surfaces and textures. Only then will you be able to look rigorously, stripping away the significance and associations of the subject so that you can see objectively. When you've learnt to see, you will be able to draw.

WHY DRAW THE FIGURE?
Until the 1960s, the ability to draw the figure competently was a primary test of artistic skill. Every art school held life classes and all students were required to attend. The thinking behind the curriculum was that if you could draw the figure you could draw anything.

The processes involved in drawing the figure are actually no different from drawing a still life group or a landscape, but our 'knowledge' of the subject and our preconceptions about the way that we look can interfere with our ability to see the figure clearly. All the skills acquired in learning to draw the figure can be applied to other subjects, so if you absorb

In this striking study of a young woman, Albany Wiseman has used black coloured pencil to establish the figure and then applied bold, black crayon for the dress. The touches of deep orange provide an eye-catching contrast.

the lessons in this book and work through the projects, you will find that not only can you tackle the figure competently and confidently, but your general draughtsmanship will also have improved.

LEARNING TO DRAW THE FIGURE
Drawing the figure is not about specific techniques such as hatching, shading, using a pen or handling a pastel. There are many amateur artists who have a wonderful technique in an array of media, but can't draw. Being able to get the best from your chosen medium is an advantage, and a beautifully handled line or a well-laid wash will add to the viewer's enjoyment of an image, but it won't make a poor drawing better, nor will it make a badly proportioned figure look convincing.

The ability to draw the figure accurately and confidently is gained from an understanding of the proportions of the figure, its structures and volumes and the extent and limitation of its movements. The exercises in this book are designed to give you that understanding.

WARM-UP EXERCISES

Before you start a drawing session, try some or all of the following warm-up exercises. They will help to dispel the fear of the blank white page and the hesitation that is inevitable when you begin.

You will need a good supply of cheap paper and some charcoal, chalk or a soft (6B or 4B) pencil – whichever medium you feel most comfortable with. Try to persuade a friend or a member of your family to pose for you. If you are really stuck for a model, you can always draw yourself in a mirror. Secure the paper to a drawing board with bulldog clips or masking tape, and position yourself comfortably.

Exercise 1: Use a single line to draw around the silhouette of the figure. Avoid the temptation to put in any details. You should end up with a continuous outline containing an empty space. If the figure is crouched, seated or kneeling, the shape may look a little strange. Now try the same exercise but don't look at the paper – keep your gaze fixed on the subject. See if the end of your line links up with the beginning of the line.

Exercise 2: Make a quick line drawing using your left hand, or your right hand if you are left-handed. Because you are engaging a different part of your brain, you will find that you bypass your normal assumptions about the figure and produce a surprisingly lively drawing.

Exercise 3: For this exercise, cut a rectangle in a sheet of paper or card and hold this up in front of you so that it frames the subject. Make sure that some parts of the figure – for example, the head and the feet in a standing pose – are cropped by the edge of the frame. Now draw the spaces which are trapped between the figure and the edge of the frame. You'll find that by drawing 'nothing', you have actually drawn the figure.

ABOUT THIS BOOK

Each section of the book deals with a basic principle, such as reducing the figure to simple geometric shapes, considering the way the bony skeleton and the soft tissues affect the appearance of the figure or drawing with line or tone. You are then invited to apply these concepts in a series of associated projects. Read through the project and then set up a similar pose. Draw the figure, applying the concepts outlined in the theory boxes and the project.

Remember that it is the process that is important, not the finished image. You often learn more by making mistakes, recognising them and righting them than by producing a

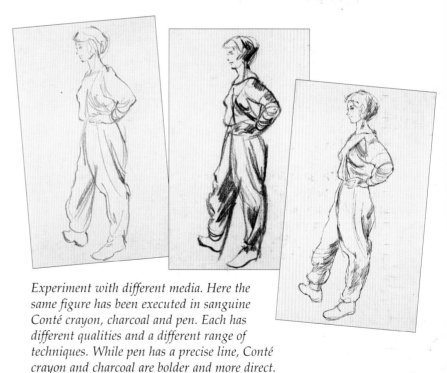

Experiment with different media. Here the same figure has been executed in sanguine Conté crayon, charcoal and pen. Each has different qualities and a different range of techniques. While pen has a precise line, Conté crayon and charcoal are bolder and more direct.

APPROACHES TO DRAWING THE FIGURE

This study was made directly using brush and watercolour. It has a force and simplicity which could not be achieved in any other way.

character, create a mood or add a splash of colour and texture. Fabrics are interesting to draw and can reveal the underlying forms or completely mask them. A large hat often creates an interesting shape on the page and can also be used to reflect a personality or tell a story.

Light is a vital component of any drawing and, by adjusting it, you can affect the amount of detail that it is possible to see and also create a specific mood (see page 64). Strong side light produces dramatic contrasts of

perfect 'finished' drawing. Practice will improve your ability to see and to draw accurately, and inevitably your manual dexterity and the skill with which you handle different media will also improve.

WORKING WITH THE MODEL

The best way of finding out about the figure is by direct observation, which means using a model. You need cooperation for subjects such as the figure in arrested motion (see pages 38–45), but often you can draw friends or family as they relax watching television or reading. Alternatively, drawing yourself in a mirror is an excellent way of making studies of particular features such as the head or hands and feet. However, if you are really to get to grips with the volumes of the figure in a variety of poses, you need to work from a model. If you can get a group

of artists together, you could hire a model or take turns to pose for the group. You can also attend a life drawing class at a local college – they offer excellent opportunities to work from the nude at very little cost.

Be considerate to your models, make sure that they are comfortable and allow them a break at regular intervals. Chalk or masking tape can be used to mark the location of the body, so that the model can easily resume the pose. And, if the pose isn't exactly the same, adjust your drawing to accommodate the changes.

When you are setting up the model's pose, think about the background and the lighting. The background can become an important element in the finished image and it can also enable you to draw more accurately (see pages 34–35). Clothes can be used to add

Pencil line and watercolour wash combine control with spontaneity. The figure is beautifully resolved, but the washes of colour give it a fresh and lively quality.

tone and dark shadows, while a more diffuse overall light allows you to see the entire figure in detail.

TYPES OF DRAWING

The human figure is uniquely flexible and expressive, and lends itself to many inter- pretations. A figure drawing may be made as an exercise, a record, an investigation, a preparation for another work, or it may be a 'finished' work in its own right. Some drawings are developed slowly over a period of time and have a cool, restrained quality while others are dashed down at great speed and retain the immediacy of the moment. The subject will affect the approach and the mood of the drawing so, for example, an informal drawing of a young child will have a different feel from a formal portrait of a dis- tinguished adult.

As you become more accom- plished and confident of your abilities, you will inevitably develop a personal drawing style. You will find that certain media suit your personality, method of working and subject matter. Nevertheless, it is a good idea to force yourself to experiment with different media and approaches from time to time – it will keep you alert and your drawings fresh. And, no matter how skilled you become, you should never abandon drawing directly from life. Even the greatest draughts- men never stopped looking and learning about the figure.

Conté crayon in a sanguine shade was used for this acutely observed and carefully rendered study of a dancer. The artist has combined a precisely drawn line with meticulous hatching, to create an image which has a classical rigour and beauty.

GALLERY

Each artist interprets the human figure in his or her own unique way, and studying these different interpretations can be fascinating, revealing and inspiring. The character of the image will be affected by the intention of the artist, the purpose of the drawing, the nature of the subject and the type of medium and support. Brush drawings in ink or watercolour have a soft and flowing quality, pastel and charcoal are bold and vigorous, while a carefully rendered drawing in hard pencil can seem cool and clinical. You will find it rewarding to study the work of other artists whenever you can, and remember that there isn't a single 'right' way of drawing the figure – there are lots of right ways.

Elsie Dressing at the Dell

John Lidzey

46 x 30cm (18 x 12in)

In this study of a figure seen *contre jour* (against the light), the cool, dim interior contrasts with the sunlight outside. A waxy black Conté pencil has been used to create a range of tones from light grey to a deep, velvety black. The white of the paper stands for bright sunlight falling on the pale, gauzy curtains.

Tom, Watching TV
Susan Pontefract
20 x 15cm (8 x 6in)

The only time children are still is when they are asleep, so you have to work fast to capture them on paper. The artist's confident handling of watercolour allowed her to capture her child's hesitant stance, the transparency of his skin and the character of his clothes and shoes with a few economical brushmarks.

Masai Warrior
John Cleal
41 x 30cm (16 x 12in)

The directness and speed with which this artist works is evident in this vigorous pen and wash study, and echoes the energy of the lean, running figure. The cropping of the figure as it moves into the picture space, and the counterpointed diagonals of the torso, limbs and spear all contribute to the pervading sense of movement.

Up Over my Head
Sarah Cawkwell
122 x 162cm (48 x 64in)

In this unusual triptych, the artist has combined close observation, meticulous detail and tight cropping to transform an everyday subject into an arresting image. She uses the linear and tonal qualities of charcoal to describe the complex patterns and textures of the woman's pullover – which in turn suggest the form beneath the clothing in a subtle but completely believable way.

Young Dancer
Michael Whittlesea
41 x 30cm (16 x 12in)

Pastel is a wonderfully flexible medium. Here, the artist combines acute observation and understanding of the figure with sensitive but bold handling of the medium. He uses a confident line to define the figure, scribbled lines for the net tutu and colour skimmed on with the side of the stick for the leg warmers. Energetically applied splashes of colour draw attention to the ballerina's head.

DRAWING IN LINE AND TONE

There are two principal ways of drawing – in line and in tone. Both methods are useful and both will help you to understand the figure in different ways. Line drawing is the most demanding of the two, because it is so economical. You have to look at the subject intensely and edit rigorously and, for this reason, line drawing is an excellent exercise for the beginner. In a tonal drawing, on the other hand, you dispense with line and simply record the areas of light and dark on a subject. Again, this method really forces you to look, and will help you to understand the bulk and roundness of the figure. But the most satisfying aspect of this approach is the ease with which even an absolute beginner can produce a convincing drawing when working in tone. The projects in this exercise introduce you to both methods and use charcoal as a drawing tool because it encourages you to work boldly and broadly.

Male, Seated
Charcoal on tinted paper
55 x 46cm (21½ x 18in)

LINE OR TONE?

The most sophisticated and demanding drawing technique is line drawing without shading. A line is a way of representing the edge of an object or a form, or the junction between areas of colour or tone. In reality, of course, there are no lines around a figure, so you have to work very hard in order to summarise the subject using this rather artificial device.

Pure outline drawing has a flat, two-dimensional quality which is often exploited in cartoons, comic illustrations and some animations. Most line drawings also include contour lines that go around and across the body, following the rise and fall of the surface to give a sense of the volumes of the form. You can also suggest depth and form by varying the quality of the line, using thin, light marks on the edges which catch the light and darker, thicker lines where an edge is in the shade. You can add tone by using hatching and stippling techniques.

The advantages of line are the speed with which you can work and the way that it forces you to distil the essence of the subject. But it is a very unforgiving technique and you'll find that, because errors and inaccuracies really show, you are forced to be rigorous. However, the best line drawings have a spare, fluid beauty which cannot be matched by any other technique.

Drawing in tone involves an entirely different process, and you will be surprised to find how easily you can produce a figure which has a convincing solidity. When light shines on a figure, the side which is turned away from the light source, or sources, will be in shadow. The areas between light and dark are called 'half-tones'. Tone describes the lightness or darkness of a thing or a colour. It is the contrast between the lights and darks and the distribution of the 'half-tones' that allows us to understand form.

Practise drawing the figure using line only, tone only and a combination of both techniques. The finished images will have very different qualities, but perhaps more importantly, each process will help you to understand better the different aspects of the figure.

This figure, drawn in pure tone using charcoal, describes the light falling on the body and the solidity of the form.

The same figure drawn in pen and ink using outline, contour lines and loosely hatched tone has a lively and expressive quality.

A LINE DRAWING EXERCISE

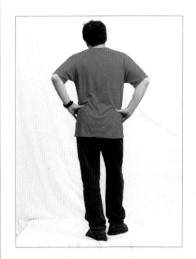

For your first line drawing, ask the model to take up a standing pose with his back turned towards you. This will avoid technical problems like foreshortening, and you won't be distracted by trying to get a facial likeness. However, you will find that back views are just as characterful as frontal views. If you can, work standing at an easel, at least 2.4m (8ft) away from the model, so that you can see the entire figure without distortion, and give yourself ten minutes for this exercise.

Materials and Equipment

• CREAM TINTED DRAWING PAPER, OR WHITE CARTRIDGE PAPER • THIN STICK OF CHARCOAL, PLUS A CHARCOAL HOLDER (OPTIONAL) • FIXATIVE

MALE, BACK VIEW

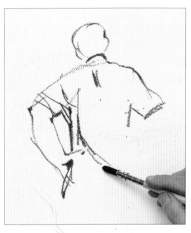

1

Position yourself so that you can look at the model and then at the drawing by simply shifting your gaze. Study the figure carefully and plot the head on the paper, checking that the entire figure will fit within the sheet. This is an outline drawing, so look for the edges of the torso and the arms. You don't need to stick to a continuous line – broken and repeated lines give the drawing a lively quality.

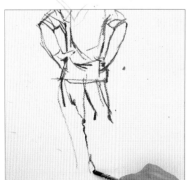

2

Look at the spaces between the arms and torso, and between the legs – if these 'negative' shapes are correct, your drawing is probably on the right lines. Draw the folds on the back of the tee-shirt, as these give a clue to the underlying forms. Vary the pressure on the charcoal to produce thick and thin lines.

3

Suit the line to the subject's character. Here, the artist has used a solid, vigorous line to suggest the heavy quality of the model's jeans. The folds in the fabric and the lines around the bottom of the trouser leg capture the heavy drape of the material. Try to mentally 'feel' the nature of the surfaces and fabrics you are drawing.

LOOKING AT DIFFERENT VIEWPOINTS

These line drawings should be made quickly, so ask the model to hold each pose for five minutes – set a timer or an alarm clock and stop drawing whether you have finished or not. After the first pose, ask the model to keep a similar stance, but to change position so that he is sideways on. Then start another drawing immediately, on the same sheet of paper. Choose simple standing poses similar to the ones shown; you will have to learn to cope with minor shifts of the head and hands, particularly if you use an inexperienced model.

MALE, FRONT AND SIDE VIEWS

1

This drawing has to be done very quickly, so take a long, hard look at the model and begin to draw the head, shoulders and torso, noting the angles they make against each other. Try to suggest that shapes continue around the image, and that the figure has another side. Don't erase lines, simply redraw them if they are incorrect.

2

Let your eyes roam around the figure, constantly checking and rechecking the relationship between one area and another – the tilt of the head, the angle of the leg, the distance between the feet. Imagine the figure beneath the clothing. Note, for example, where the knees should be, and see how this point relates to the folds in the fabric.

Materials and Equipment

• CREAM TINTED DRAWING PAPER, OR WHITE CARTRIDGE PAPER • THIN STICK OF CHARCOAL, PLUS A CHARCOAL HOLDER (OPTIONAL) • FIXATIVE

3

Ask the model to turn to the side and adopt exactly the same pose as before. Start another drawing on the same sheet of paper if there is room. Take a deep breath and plunge in. Start with the head, establishing the slope of the jaw and the eyes, and the angle of the neck. Notice the way the neck sits into the front of the shoulders and projects forwards. Establish the angles of the upper arm and forearm, the curve of the shoulder and the sleeve. The best way to give volume to your figure is to 'feel' the shapes as you draw them. Concentrate on their roundness, solidity and bulk.

4

Establish the line of the legs, then use a bolder line to capture the drape of the heavy jean fabric.

5

Drawing with line only will force you to edit and decide what is really important. The figures have been simplified so that only the most essential features are shown. Notice how the creases in the jeans help to establish the character of the fabric, while the seams convey the structure of the garment as well as the form beneath. Lightly spray the finished drawing with fixative in a well-ventilated room or outdoors.

AN EXERCISE IN TONE

For this tonal exercise, you need a strongly lit figure, so place the model by a window or use a spotlight to direct light from one side. A seated pose provides interesting shapes and interlocking areas of light and dark.

Materials and Equipment

• SHEET OF CREAM TINTED DRAWING PAPER, OR WHITE CARTRIDGE PAPER • THIN STICKS OF CHARCOAL, PLUS A CHARCOAL HOLDER (OPTIONAL) • FIXATIVE

MALE, SEATED

1

At first, it can be difficult to see tone because colours, patterns and reflected light cause confusion. If you screw up your eyes, you will find it easier to see the distribution of lights and darks across the surface. Start by simplifying the tones, looking for the lightest and darkest areas. Use the tip of the charcoal to hatch in the dark tones on the back of the head and torso, noting the dark shadow that the head casts on to the shoulder.

2

Continue hatching in the dark tones, allowing them to travel around the form. Put in patches of dark tone on the face, the forearm and the torso. If you draw exactly what you see, you will find that features and forms begin to emerge as if by magic from the jigsaw of light and dark shapes. Use brisk, spiky marks where the thigh is in shadow to suggest the pull of the fabric.

3

Add areas of darker tone around the waist, on the inside of the far leg, on the trousers and on the back of the foot. Place a sheet of paper under your hand to prevent smudging, if you wish. Continue surveying the figure through half-closed eyes, comparing the tones across it. Look for areas that are the same tone and check that the contrasts between areas of light and dark are correct. Draw exactly what you see rather than what you 'know' to be there. This exercise is about pure observation.

4

Block in the areas of dark and mid tone on the shoes and the crate on which the model is sitting. Stand back and assess your drawing from a distance, comparing it with the subject. Use an extra-thin stick of charcoal to add details like the seam on the trousers, the shadows and creases on the trousers, and the darkest tones on the hair and face.

5

Your eyes should travel from model to drawing and from one part of the drawing to another, constantly assessing the tonal values. Work across the entire drawing, making adjustments here and there. Cast shadows are important, because they provide information about the surface on to which they fall, and about the direction and quality of light. Here, the shadows establish the horizontal surface of the floor, and they are dark and crisp because the light is strong and directional.

6

You will probably be surprised to find how easy it is to create an accurate, solid and convincing figure drawing by organising the areas of light, dark and mid tone accurately. Practise working in this way whenever you can – you will soon develop a feel for the volumes of the figure and this will be carried into all your drawings and paintings.

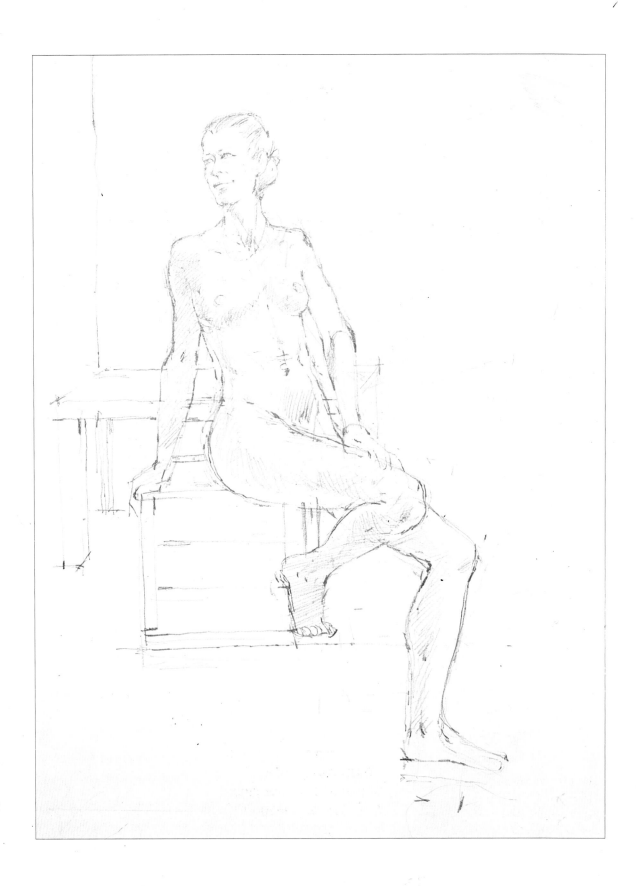

DRAWING ACCURATELY

Based on close observation, 'objective' drawing is analytical and enquiring. This approach allows the artist to discover and describe the appearance of the subject, and to create an illusion of three dimensions on a two-dimensional support. It is the foundation of all traditional Western art. Learning to draw anything, whether it is the figure or a cup and saucer, is really about learning to look and see. That sounds simple, but unfortunately we are often led astray by what we 'think' we remember about the human form. So we know that legs and arms are cylindrical, the head sits on top of the shoulders and the hand consists of four separate fingers and a thumb. But, if they are seen in perspective, legs and arms cease to be cylinders, the head actually projects from the front of the shoulders, and the hand is often seen as a single, compact shape. Drawing from life forces you to look again, to question every mark, and to unlearn what you think you know.

Seated Nude
Graphite on watercolour paper
56 x 38cm (22 x 15in)

IMPROVE YOUR ACCURACY

The impact of an objective drawing depends on the accuracy with which you reproduce the image. Your pencil can be used to take precise measurements, to check proportions and angles, and to transfer this information to the drawing (see photographs below). Keep your arm straight to maintain a constant distance between the pencil and your eye.

To check relative proportions of the body, hold a pencil vertically out in front of you, closing one eye. Align the top of the pencil with a key point, then slide your thumb down to align with another key point.

Another useful technique to maintain accuracy is to look for vertical and horizontal lines and alignments, and see which parts of the body a line would pass through or touch if it were extended. The centre of the face, the centre of the front torso and the spine are key lines, so indicate their location and see where they fall in relation to the shoulders, limbs and background.

You can also use edges in the background to locate the figure. If the model is standing in front of a door or a window, for example, notice where architectural points impinge upon the figure and pay special attention to lines that appear on either side of it.

Negative spaces are spaces between and around the figure or other objects. Study them carefully, noticing their precise shapes, and draw those rather than the 'positive' shapes. Because negative shapes are abstract, you will be more objective and will draw what you actually see rather than what you assume you know, so you are likely to build up a more accurate figure with a pleasingly uncontrived quality.

If you are worried about the proportions of a drawing, try turning it on its head – this gives you a new viewpoint, helping you to see flaws to which your eye has become accustomed. Reversing the image in a mirror has a similar effect. And remember to stand back from your drawing from time to time so that you can view it from a distance.

Left: Once you have established a measurement between two key points, such as the top of the head and the chin, you can check this against other body measurements.

Right: With your arm extended, lay the pencil along the slope of the shoulders to check the angle. Transfer that angle to the paper.

PROPORTIONS OF THE FIGURE

Because we take our own form for granted, drawing the figure can be full of surprises. We tend to assume the head is bigger than it is and the hands and feet are smaller, so it can be disconcerting to find that the hand covers the face from chin to hairline, and the foot is a similar length to the head.

The other revelation is the sheer diversity of the human form. There are the obvious differences between male and female, and adults and children, but you'll find that there are variations in height, body weight, shoulder width and length of leg, too. Nevertheless, it is useful to work with a set of ideal

The hand covers the face from the chin almost to the hairline.

proportions, because most people can be fitted into the standard pattern with some adjustments.

In the 'average' human, the head fits into the standing figure approximately seven to eight times. The upper torso, from waist to the neck, is about two heads high and the pelvis about one head high. The legs are approximately the same length as the head and trunk, with the thighs and the lower legs being about two heads each. If the arms are hanging by the side, the tips of the fingers will reach halfway down the thigh. The shoulders are about three heads wide and the pelvis is about one-and-a-half heads wide.

In general, the female figure differs slightly from the male. In the male the hips are narrower than the shoulders, whereas in the female they are about the same width. In the female the pelvis is longer, but the legs are shorter.

A baby's head is large in proportion to the rest of the body. Throughout childhood, the rest of the body grows much more than the head, so that by adulthood, the figure's proportions have radically changed.

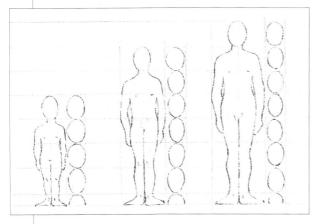

At a year old, a child's head is still quite large in proportion to the rest of the body. The legs are relatively short, so the centre point of the figure falls at the stomach.

By eight years' old, the head has enlarged slightly and the legs have lengthened so that the mid-point of the body now falls just above the hips.

In the average adult, the head fits into the body approximately seven-and-a-half times. The legs account for about half the height of the figure.

A VISUAL REFERENCE

Use a piece of furniture or an architectural feature as a reference against which to plot a figure drawing. Here, an easel provides a support for the model as well as a grid of lines to assist the drawing process. A plumb line has been pinned to the backdrop to give a useful vertical.

Materials and Equipment

- SHEET OF NOT WATERCOLOUR PAPER
- HB PENCIL

STANDING NUDE

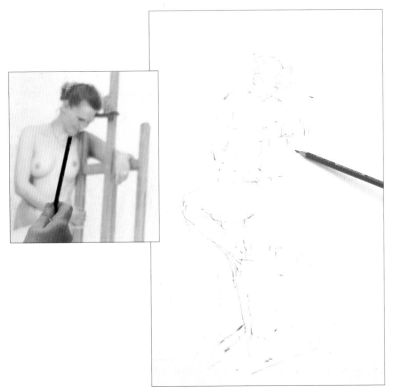

1

The angles of the model's torso and the upright of the easel are key elements of this study, so use your pencil to measure both these angles (see inset) and transfer them to the paper. Measure the slope of the shoulder, the thigh and the horizontal struts of the easel and lightly tick them in. Note the points at which the easel meets the model's body, and the angle between the figure and the plumb line. Measure the model's head and see how many times it fits into the body – just over seven times. These measurements provide a solid foundation for the drawing. Start to sketch in the figure, working lightly.

2

Check the height of the vertical strut of the easel: the distance between the top and the first horizontal is the same as that between the horizontal and the ledge. If you get these measurements right, the figure is more likely to look correct.

3

Continue developing the drawing, trying to get a broad feel for the pose. Allow your eye to travel over the figure to check horizontal and vertical relationships. Note that the angle of the model's right leg mirrors the angle of the supporting struts of the easel, and the bar she is leaning on aligns with her nipples.

4

Let the model rest from time to time – use chalk or masking tape to mark the position of the feet and hands so that she can resume the pose. If the pose is slightly different after the break, make adjustments to your drawing. The feet are important to the logic of the drawing, so draw them carefully.

5

When you are satisfied that the figure is accurately established, start to add details such as the hands and face. Half-close your eyes and look for the light and shadow. Hatch areas of tone on the stomach, under the breasts, on the thigh and on the raised foot. Finally, apply a tone to the hair, allowing the hatching to describe the way the hair grows.

ARRANGING A SEATED POSE

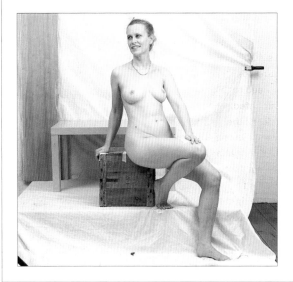

Experiment before you settle on a seated pose. This pose presents the figure as an extended diagonal, with the legs making a series of angles. The props were arranged to produce interesting negative shapes, and horizontal and vertical lines against which to measure the figure. Because the pose is somewhat complex, it is important to mark key positions with masking tape.

SEATED NUDE

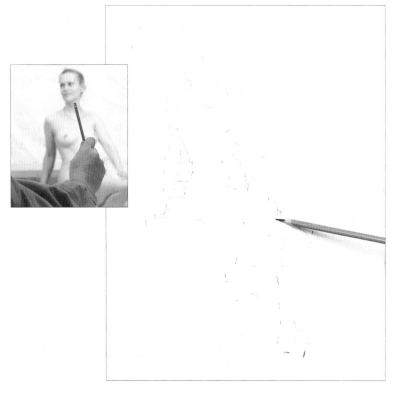

Materials and Equipment

• SHEET OF NOT WATERCOLOUR PAPER
• HB PENCIL

1

Use a pencil to find the angle of the seated figure (see inset), as this is the key to the entire pose. Mark this slope on the paper. Draw the head, indicating the centre line, and check that the angle is correct. Lightly sketch in the horizontals and verticals in the background. Begin to outline the figure, looking for the points at which it meets the background. Check the 'negative' shapes between the arms and the torso, and the angular shapes delimited by the legs.

2

Draw the model and the crate on which she is sitting as a single entity. The seated figure does not support itself, so you need to explain how the weight is distributed. Here, the model is taking a lot of the weight on her right hand. Start to add the dark tones on the right arm and under the right breast. Notice that the artist has indicated how the left leg passes behind the right leg – the drawing will be more convincing if you understand what is happening to the hidden parts of the figure.

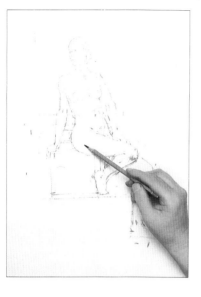

3

Begin to refine details such as the head and hands. Lay in loosely hatched tone on the torso, following the curves of the form. Draw the far leg of the small table – the obvious perspective creates a sense of space in the drawing. Block in a dark tone on the shin of the near leg.

4

Develop the model's head by applying tone under the chin and the lower lip, on the hair and behind the jawbone. Complete the drawing by adding hatched tone on the calves, around the upper thigh and on the inside of the left arm.

THE MOVING FIGURE

Capturing the figure in motion is a challenge, even for the most accomplished artist. You must learn to draw quickly and capture the essence of a gesture or a movement in a few fluid lines. This is much easier if you simplify the forms in your mind, seeing the figure as a series of solid geometric shapes which articulate against each other in predictable ways. If you practise drawing rapidly from life, you will develop a shorthand which allows you to express movement with a few telling strokes. The projects in this exercise involve drawing from the model, freezing movements mid-action in a way that rarely occurs in real life. These short poses will give you a greater understanding of the figure in motion. Avoid detail, concentrate on how the weight of the body is distributed, and look for lines that imply that the movement will be continued.

Striding Out
Hard pastel on cartridge paper
44 x 35cm (17¼ x 13¾in)

SIMPLIFYING THE FIGURE

To draw a convincing figure, you must create the illusion of a solid form in space. A useful way of understanding the solidity of the figure is to reduce the component forms to geometric shapes. The head can be seen as a sphere, the arms and legs as tapering cylinders, the torso and pelvis as modified cylinders or cubes, and the hands and feet as basically cubic shapes. Because these shapes are simple and familiar, it is easy to visualise them tilted, overlapping or in perspective. If you use them as the basis for a drawing and then apply your knowledge of proportion and the underlying structures, you will be able to draw a solid figure in any position.

If you imagine the human figure as a doll made up of these geometric shapes joined by elastic, you will begin to understand the way in which the different parts articulate against one another and this will give you an insight into the figure in motion. These 'manikins' can be fleshed out to produce a convincing nude or clothed figure. They are also a useful way of investigating what is going on in a difficult pose before you start a drawing.

The dancer in this pose (above left) is poised and erect, her weight resting on one buttock, while her legs are very slightly braced against the bench, the floor and each other. The manikin figure (right) reveals the relationship of the main elements of the figure and shows how the legs articulate around the knee joint.

The swing of the pelvis and the slight bend in the left leg are the key to this pose, as shown in the manikin figure.

CAPTURING MOVEMENT

Drawing the moving figure requires many skills. You must be able to simplify the forms, find the lines that sum up the movement and commit poses to memory so that you can complete the drawing when the moment has passed. Above all, practise, work quickly and don't be afraid of making 'mistakes'.

Begin by persuading a friend to model for a series of short poses. Ask her to walk around the room and then stop suddenly, freezing a movement. Start with five-minute poses and reduce the time as you become more proficient. If you want to sketch people going about activities such as shopping or playing sports, you need to get something down in about ten seconds.

Work on a large sheet of paper and use a medium such as charcoal, chalk or pastel which allows you to work freely and boldly. Ideally, stand at an easel – this encourages you to use big

Do a series of quick warm-up exercises on a sheet of paper. Short poses force you to reject non-essential information and focus on the key directions and rhythms.

movements from the elbow and the shoulder, rather than finicky gestures from the wrist. Study the pose carefully and then start to draw, looking for the direction of the motion, the distribution of weight and the centre of gravity. If some of your lines are inaccurate, simply redraw them. The build-up of lines will suggest movement and vitality.

Apply the three-dimensional forms of the manikin figure as you draw. Use ellipses and contours to suggest the volumes of limbs and torso, and visualise what is happening on the far side of the figure. Try to understand the logic behind the pose, the action of the joints and how compression in one area is balanced by stretching in another.

POSES SHOWING MOVEMENT

Ask the model to move around and then stop mid-movement. Allow a maximum of five minutes for each of the poses.

Materials and Equipment
- SHEET OF CREAM CANSON PAPER
- CONTÉ CRAYON: SANGUINE

GIRL, TURNING

1

Look for the way the figure is balanced – here the weight is on the model's right leg while her body swings around to the right, pivoting at the waist. Work quickly, feeling the flow of the movement and the rhythms of the pose. Simplify the shapes, using an oval for the head and cylinders for the limbs and trunk. In that way, you will capture the volume of the figure.

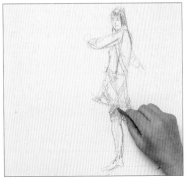

2

Once you have captured the essence of the pose, start to add superficial details such as the hair, the pattern on the skirt and the dark tone where the knee is in shadow. Indicate the folds in the sleeve – these contours suggest the roundness and foreshortening of the arms.

3

The finished sketch captures the energy of the pose. Short poses force you to be selective, and this is good practice for working on location when you have no control over the model.

Girl, Turning, Back View

1

Ask the model to turn and 'freeze' another gesture. Look for the line that expresses the main thrust of the pose – in this case, the line down the left side of the figure. Indicate the angle of the shoulders and hips. These are critical as they change as the weight shifts from one leg to the other. Work quickly, looking for the main thrusts and tensions. These mid-movement poses are difficult to hold, so be prepared to adjust the drawing as the model shifts.

2

Begin to add more emphatic lines, firming up the outlines of the legs and arms, and refining details such as the pattern on the skirt and the hair, all the time searching for the forms and the sense of an implied movement. Allow your gaze to switch back and forth between the model and the drawing.

3

The finished drawing is simple, direct and energetic. The redundant construction lines emphasise the immediacy and energy of the drawing.

STRETCHING AND BENDING

Ask the model to take up a pose that she can hold for at least five minutes. To find interesting and realistic poses, ask her to move around and then tell her to freeze.

Materials and Equipment
- SHEET OF WHITE CARTRIDGE PAPER
- BLACK CHARCOAL PENCIL
- HARD PASTELS: PINK, FLESH TINT, BURNT SIENNA, SAGE GREEN, LEMON YELLOW, BLUE AND ORANGE

GIRL, STRETCHING

1

Use a charcoal pencil to sketch the figure. Forget about detail and concentrate on the proportions and position of the body. Try to see the figure as the linked geometric shapes described on page 40. With the pencil, check the relative positions of key elements such as the head, the waist and the knees. Work boldly, using quick gestural marks that follow the stresses and tensions of the pose.

2

Using a pink pastel stick, describe the folds on the sleeves and the back of the model's blouse. Rub flesh tint on to the hands and the legs, and add burnt sienna for the shadows on the legs. Use the pink, sage green, lemon yellow and blue pastels to complete the pattern on the skirt.

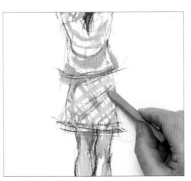

3

The vigorous finished drawing captures the essence of the stretching figure perfectly. The lively lines reflect the speed with which it was made.

GIRL, BENDING

1

Using a charcoal pencil, indicate the main rhythms of the pose. Work quickly with flowing lines that follow the direction of the movement. Look for the telling lines: here, they are the curve of the model's back and the line of the right, supporting leg. Don't use an eraser, simply redraw inaccurate lines – multiple lines and a blurred outline all add to the sense of movement.

3

Complete the skirt plaid with blue, sage green and lemon yellow pastel. Use burnt sienna for the shadows on the model's legs and for her bag. Add a touch of orange where the bag catches the light. The finished image captures the essence of the movement with great economy.

2

Suggest the colour of the blouse and the skirt plaid with a few brisk strokes of pink pastel, using the side of the stick to block in general colour and the tip to lay in the folds and stripes. These swinging lines are wonderfully energetic and enhance the sense of motion in the drawing. Apply flesh tint on the face, hands and legs, warming it with a little pink.

Exercise

4

BONES, MUSCLE AND BALANCE

Abasic understanding of anatomy – in particular, of the skeleton and the muscle groups and how they change with every action – will enable you to draw the nude and clothed figure with confidence and conviction. The way that fabric drapes around the figure is largely dependent on what is going on underneath – a good drawing should make you aware of the figure under the clothing. The skeleton provides a rigid framework and is overlaid by muscles and fatty tissue, the whole package contained in an envelope of skin. In some places, the bony structures are near the surface and determine the form; in others, it is the soft tissues that create the contours. These are also the factors that create the differences in shape between individuals, men and women, adults and children. If the figure is to stay erect, the muscles must work against each other, keeping the body in balance. Capturing these often fleeting moments of equilibrium is important if a drawing is to look stable and convincing.

Girl, Standing
50 x 33 cm (19 x 13in)

Girl, Sitting
51 x 56cm (20 x 22in)

*Graphite and water-soluble
coloured pencils*

THE SKELETON

The skeleton is a lightweight framework of bones, held together by muscle, cartilage and tendons. From the artist's point of view, the spinal column is the most important structure as it is the axis around which the other bones are grouped and its position is the key to many poses.

The most notable feature of the spinal column is its flexibility. It isn't straight, but curves out in the shoulder area, inwards towards the waist and out again over the pelvis before tucking in and out at the coccyx. These curves act as shock absorbers and define many aspects of posture.

Although there is only a little movement between one vertebra and the next, the cumulative effect over the entire length of the spine allows for bending backwards, forwards and side to side, plus twisting movements. These movements are made possible by the powerful muscles of the back.

The top part of the skeleton consists of the ribcage, at the top of which the hoop of collar bones and shoulder blades provides an attachment for the arms. The pelvic girdle, attached to the lower end of the spine, is a heavy and fairly rigid structure designed to carry the weight of the upper body and allow it to be supported on the lower limbs.

The limbs consist of long bones. The upper arm fits into a shallow socket in the shoulder blade and the two slim bones in the lower arm meet the upper arm at the elbow joint.

The rounded heads of the thigh bones sit in deep sockets in the pelvis. Note that the hip joints are on the outside of the pelvis, so that the thigh bones slope in towards the knees – this effect is more pronounced in women who tend to have wider pelvic bones.

The skull is balanced on top of the spine. All its plate-like bones are fused except the lower jaw bone which articulates against the rest of the structure from points just in front of the ears.

The hands and feet are complex structures consisting of many tiny bones. The hand is heavily jointed to provide maximum flexibility, while the foot bones are wedged tightly together and bound with ligaments to give the foot both flexibility and strength.

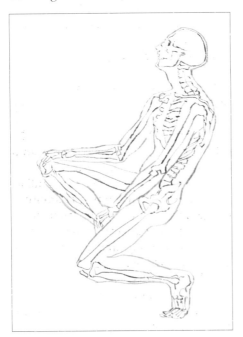

The skeleton provides the basic architecture of the body and gives it a solid underpinning.

THE SOFT TISSUES

The bony skeleton defines the broad structures and dimensions of the body, but the appearance of the figure is also determined by layers of muscle and fatty tissue. In some places the muscular tissue is bulky and dominates the surface area, while in others, bones come close to the surface.

Muscles work in pairs, providing power and leverage for the body. The musculature of the body is complex, consisting of layers of large and small muscles which perform specific tasks. Although you can draw the figure effectively without becoming an expert on anatomy, you should be aware of the way that some muscles affect the shape and surface forms of the figure.

The upper part of the torso is quite bony in character. If you run your hands over that area, you will find that the collar bone, breast bone, ribs and the bones in the shoulder are only thinly covered. The area between the rib cage and the pelvis is soft and fleshy and is capable of considerable movement. Notice the furrow that runs down the front of the torso to the base of the rib cage, and the fleshy mound of the abdomen. The pectoral muscles emanate from the breast bone and insert into the shoulder – in women they are partially masked by the breasts.

On the back, a furrow runs the entire length of the spine, with the powerful muscles of the back radiating out from this line. The fleshiest part of the back is the buttocks, which are formed by several muscles.

When the arm is flexed, the biceps and deltoid muscles bulge and become more apparent. The form of the legs is

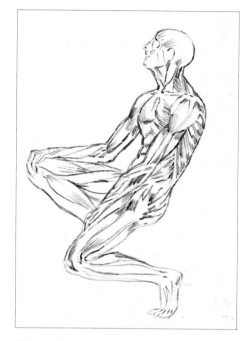

The skeleton is enveloped in layers of muscle and other soft tissue that smooth the outline and create fleshy masses in certain areas of the body.

defined to a large extent by the hard-working muscles that almost entirely mask the thigh bones and create the typical rounding on the back of the calves. At the front of the leg, the shin bone is relatively unprotected.

The most convenient way of familiarising yourself with human anatomy is by getting to know your own body. Run your hands over your arms or make some exaggerated movements and notice the way that the muscles lengthen or bulge. Stand in front of a mirror in a strong light and observe the fleshy masses on the abdomen, buttocks, arms and legs.

A Pose in Equilibrium

Ask the model to stand with her weight on her left leg and her hand on her hip. Automatically, the left hip will swing out and up, and the other hip will drop down. The shoulder on the left side will also drop slightly. These adjustments all help to keep the body in balance.

Materials and Equipment

- SHEET OF CARTRIDGE PAPER
- 7B PENCIL ● WATER-SOLUBLE COLOURED PENCILS: PINK, ORANGE, RAW UMBER, FLESH TINT, VENETIAN RED, CRIMSON

Girl, Standing

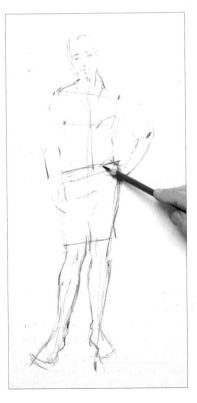

1

Using a 7B pencil, start by establishing the central axis and the opposing slant of the shoulders and hips. These angles give you the structure of the pose. Try adopting the pose yourself and notice how one part of the body acts as a counterweight to the other.

2

Develop the drawing with vigorous lines, keeping in mind the model's underlying forms. Simplify the main elements – the arms are cylinders, the legs are tapering cylinders and the knees are convex domes on the surface of the leg. Use heavier lines and scribbled shading for areas of dark tone. Develop the facial features and hatch some light shading to give the face form.

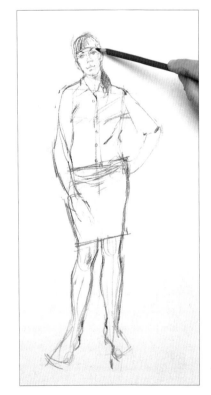

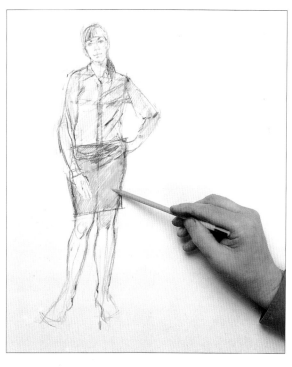

3

Using water-soluble coloured pencils, hatch pink on the blouse and a combination of orange and raw umber on the skirt. Soften the coloured pencil marks in places by blending them with a little water applied with a brush or with the tip of your finger.

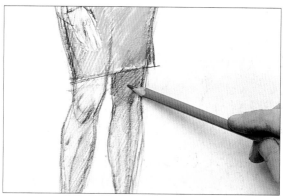

4

Apply a light flesh tint on the face, hands and legs, and warm the inside of the calves with a little Venetian red. Add shadow at the top of the leg in raw umber. Don't overwork the coloured pencil – the white paper shining through the hatching has a lively, shimmering quality which solidly applied colour would lack.

5

Refine the drawing a little further by adding more detail to the face – a touch of flesh tint on the cheek that is catching the light, some crisp detail in 7B pencil around the eyes and mouth, and a touch of crimson on the lips. While the face should capture the character of the individual, it is important that it remains in harmony with the rest of the drawing.

LOOKING AT BALANCE

Balance is important even in the seated figure. In this pose, the spine curves to the side but the head remains over the centre of gravity. Use masking tape or chalk to record the model's position.

Materials and Equipment

- SHEET OF NOT WATERCOLOUR PAPER • 7B PENCIL
- COLOURED PENCILS: BURNT UMBER, PINK, FLESH TINT, DARK BLUE, GREEN, CRIMSON, VENETIAN RED, YELLOW

GIRL, SITTING

1

Using a 7B pencil, block in the outlines of the main segments of the body: head, ribcage, pelvis and limbs. Note the location of the spine as this is the key to the pose, and notice, too, how the left side of the body is extended while the right is compressed. The legs present a challenge in perspective as the thighs project forwards. If you check relative measurements with your pencil and draw what you see, you will draw the foreshortening accurately.

2

Develop the drawing, looking for the relationships between one part of the body and another – the way that the head is balanced above the torso, for example, and the point at which a line extended from the head would meet the floor. Try to visualise the skeletal underpinning – the tilt of the shoulders and pelvis, and the foreshortening in the ribcage. A hard line suggests the tension in the muscles of the left arm and shoulder, while a softer line is used for the relaxed right arm.

3

Indicate the shadows and folds on the blouse, and the way the pattern on the skirt curves around the thighs. Details such as seams, cuffs and hems provide clues to the underlying structures. Add dark tone on the hair and warm it with a touch of burnt umber. Apply pink to the skirt and blouse, changing the direction of the marks to follow the surface planes or the tension on the cloth.

4

Lightly hatch flesh tint on to the face, hands and legs. Elaborate the pattern on the skirt with dark blue and green coloured pencils. Note how the lines rise and fall as they travel across the undulations of the thighs, revealing the underlying forms.

5

Develop the face with touches of burnt umber, flesh tint and crimson. Use flesh tint, raw umber and Venetian red for the skin tones on the leg, using the pencil marks to indicate how the surface planes change direction. Complete the plaid pattern on the skirt, add a touch of yellow to the cushion, and lightly hatch in the shadow cast by the model. Although the pose appears complicated, it is simple to draw if you combine an understanding of the underlying structures with careful observation.

HEADS, HANDS AND FEET

The head is the part of the body that most expresses the individuality of a person. For beginners, the need to find a likeness can be daunting. However, if you understand the basic structures, then look hard and measure, you will find that not only is it easy to produce a convincing image, you can also get a good likeness. The basic proportions of the head are illustrated on the following page. Study them and then observe your own face in a mirror.

Hands can also present a problem for the less experienced artist, but if you look carefully, reduce them to basic shapes and work from life, you will soon be able to draw hands that are three-dimensional, convincing and expressive. In this study, the artist started by treating the hands as simple shapes, adding details, tone and colour as the rest of the drawing progressed.

Feet, too, are easy to draw if you understand their volumes and underlying structures. Because hands and feet are quite complicated shapes, there is a temptation to put in too much detail which upsets the balance of the drawing. In this study, the hands and feet are indicated with a few deft touches and sit comfortably within the composition.

Girl on a Settee
Water-soluble pencil
40 x 40cm (15 x 15in)

LOOKING AT HEADS

The skull is a bony structure to which the facial features are attached. The eyes are spheres embedded in the hollows of the eye sockets. They are surrounded by the eyelids, the upper lid being more apparent than the lower lid. When drawing the upper eyelid, use a heavy line to indicate the thickness of the lid, and a shadow under the lower lid to suggest the depth of the lid and its angle to the cheek.

The nose is a wedge jutting out from the face. It is narrow at the top and flares out to a wide base. The bone of the nose stops short of its tip which is soft and fleshy; some noses come to a shapely tip, others are bulbous. When drawing the face from the front, a touch of shadow under the nose will make it seem to project from the face. The appearance of the nose changes as the face dips forwards or tilts backwards, and this movement also affects how much of the nostrils is visible.

The mouth is an expressive feature which gives a face much of its character. It is also an important clue to mood. The bottom lip is lighter in tone than the upper lip because its plane faces up to the light. A touch of shadow under the bottom lip will help to give it form. In profile, the upper lip tends to jut forward beyond the lower lip.

The ears can only be seen fully from the side, so usually they are seen in perspective. They equal the nose in length, aligning with its base and top.

The chin is a convex mass on the surface of the head, creating a furrow between it and the lower lip. The chin, which varies from person to person, is another important defining characteristic.

The head is basically an egg-shape with the broader end at the crown, the nose providing a central axis. The eyes are positioned half-way between the chin and the top of the head and are about an eye-width apart. The eyebrow aligns with the top of the ear and the nose is about the same depth as the forehead. The lines of the eyebrow, eyes, nose and mouth tilt as the head is lifted or lowered.

DRAWING HANDS AND FEET

Hands are flexible and complex structures. You will find it easier to tackle them if you reduce them to simple shapes. Look for the basic structures – the roughly five-sided shape of the palm, the two separate masses of the hand proper and the thumb, and the planes of the clenched fist. Move your hand and notice the range of wrist movements, Lay your hand and arm flat on a table and you'll see that the hand is broader at the fingers than at the wrist and that the wrist slants up from the hand to join the arm. When the hand is fully extended, the fingers converge to a point below the middle finger.

Make a series of drawings of your own hands in different positions. A mirror will extend the possible viewpoints. Simplify the shapes, trying to see the hand as a single unit rather than an assemblage of different elements. Place the hand you are drawing in a strong light – the shadows and highlights will reveal the surfaces and contours. Use straight, hatched lines for the planes and curved shading for the curved surfaces.

If you stretch your hand fully, you will see that the tips and joints of the fingers lie along a series of curved lines, and the thumb aligns with the

Sketch your own hand in as many different positions as possible. The model hand (bottom right) articulates at the joints and is a useful drawing aid.

second joint. Keep these relationships in mind as you are drawing.

The foot is perfectly designed for movement and support. Study the sole and note the points of contact with the ground – the heel, the ball, the toes and the outside rim. The ankle is higher on the inside of the leg than the outside, and the top of the foot forms a plane which splays out and slopes down from the inner ankle and instep.

Use a mirror to make a sheet of drawings of your own bare feet from as many different angles as possible. Notice the relationship of the foot to the leg and how the shape of the foot changes as you shift your weight.

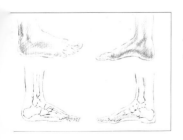

Seen from one side, the foot is in contact with the floor along its entire edge, but the inside edge is raised over the arch.

A SEATED POSE

Ask the model to sit with her feet up on a settee or bench and her arms clasped around her knees. This pose has many advantages: the model is comfortable, the flexed arms and legs make interesting angles, and the hands and feet are clearly visible. Costume and colour are an important part of a figure study. Here, the crimson blouse and cushions provide a vibrant contrast to the blue trousers, the delicate colours of the hair and skin, and the cane of the settee.

GIRL ON A SETTEE

Materials and Equipment

• SHEET OF NOT WATERCOLOUR PAPER • WATER-SOLUBLE COLOURED PENCILS: BURNT SIENNA, CRIMSON, ORANGE, DARK BLUE, GREY, LIGHT BLUE, SEPIA, CARMINE, YELLOW OCHRE, INDIAN RED, FLESH TINT • NO.3 WATERCOLOUR BRUSH

1

Decide how you are going to position the image within the support. This pose produces an almost square composition. Start to draw with a burnt sienna water-soluble pencil, working lightly but freely. Use your pencil to check proportions and angles, especially the slope of the arms, legs and back, and the tilt of the head. Tick in the line of the eyes, the mouth and the centre of the head.

2

Develop the drawing with the same burnt sienna pencil. Use light lines while you are searching for the image and more emphatic lines once you are sure that you have got it right. You can also vary the weight of the line to reflect the character of the edge you are drawing – use crisp, dark lines between areas of highly contrasted light and dark such as the hairline, the collar and the opening of the blouse and lighter lines for folds in the fabric. Add more detail to the head – the dark tone under the nose and chin and between the lips, for example. Lightly indicate the pupils.

3

Apply hatched tone on the shaded side of the face and neck. Sketch the hands with a few lightly applied lines, suggesting the location of the knuckles and the individual fingers. Shade the fingers of the left hand, treating them as a single block of tone. To render the shiny, reflective surface of the satin blouse you will need a selection of cool and warm reds, leaving the white of the paper to stand for the highlights. Use a crimson water-soluble pencil to apply loosely hatched patches of colour in the darkest areas of the fabric.

4

It is good practice to advance all areas of the drawing at the same pace, so apply some crimson to the cushion and add touches of orange to the blouse. Use the burnt sienna pencil to indicate the shadow under the left forearm, then start to block in the dark blue of the trousers.

5

Study the feet carefully and then use the burnt sienna pencil to refine the drawing. Notice the way the feet slope down from the ankle and then flatten out into the toes. Indicate the areas of tone under the ankle, between the legs, and along the edge of the foot. When you are satisfied that the drawing is correct, draw a more definite outline with the burnt sienna pencil.

6

Use a grey pencil with a sharp point to draw the eyebrows, the edge of the upper eyelid and the pupil. Use a light blue pencil for the irises. Indicate the outline of the settee with a sepia pencil, then add colour to the red cushion with the crimson pencil.

7

Add touches of carmine to the blouse. Apply a little colour to the hair with a yellow ochre pencil, then use the same colour to hatch a light tone on the forehead, the cheeks and the neck. Use the grey pencil to define the hairline and shaded area under the hair. Dip a No.3 watercolour brush in water and use it to soften and blend the colour on the face and neck – don't overdo this. While the brush is still loaded with this colour, apply a delicate wash to the left arm and hand.

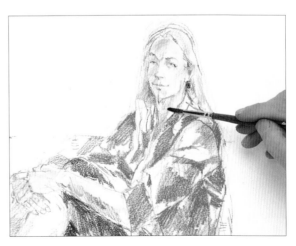

8

Work Indian red into the red of the blouse, then add touches of grey for the darkest areas. Allow the drawing to dry and then hatch flesh tint on the arm and on the face. Apply yellow and orange to those areas of the cushion that are catching the light. Hatch grey on the cushion the model is sitting on. Use yellow ochre to scribble some local colour on to the cane settee, then return to the grey pencil for the cast shadow on the wall behind the settee.

9

Dip the No.3 watercolour brush in water and start to blend the blue of the trousers and some of the hatched areas of the blouse. Don't overdo the blending – it is the combination of line and wash which gives this medium its attractive quality. Water-soluble coloured pencils are really best for small areas of wash or for softening lines. If you want to use the full range of watercolour effects, choose watercolour paint.

10

Use the sepia pencil to suggest the leg of the settee and the weave of the caning. You could leave the picture at this stage, or use the grey pencil to add a light overall tone to the background. In the final image, the figure of the girl is accurately drawn and beautifully rendered in a combination of hatched pencil techniques and blended washes. The various shapes, textures and blocks of colour also work as an abstract composition.

LIGHTING THE FIGURE

Light is the means by which you discern forms in the world about you, but it also allows you to introduce atmosphere into a drawing or painting. Light is an integral part of the subject in a figure study, establishing a mood, holding disparate elements together, emphasising forms here, rendering them ambiguous there. Change the lighting and you change every aspect of the image. A bright spotlight shining on to a figure creates contrasts of tone and a sense of drama, while softly dappled light and flickering shadows produce a quieter, more mysterious mood. Bright light casts crisp shadows, while the shadows cast by diffuse light have softer, less defined edges. Artists often use backlighting to combine drama and mystery in a study. By placing a figure against a window, as shown left, the silhouette is revealed, often with great clarity, while the rest of the figure is cast into a shadow. This near-silhouette effect is called *contre jour*.

Seated Woman, *Contre Jour*
Pastel pencil and hard pastel on tinted paper
55 x 38cm (21 x 15in)

LEARNING TO USE LIGHT

When you are setting up a figure study, it is important to consider how the light will affect the composition and the mood you want to achieve. For an investigative drawing, you will need a combination of light sources – an over-all light so that you can see the entire figure, with a side light to reveal the surface forms with greater clarity. But if you want to create a more intriguing image, you could choose to illuminate the figure from behind or with a directional light from one side. With the more exaggerated light effects, the shadows become an increasingly important element in the composition.

Daylight is generally preferred by artists because it shows colours at their truest. If you are working by natural light, remember that it will change throughout the day, so you either have to work quickly, make a few reference sketches or photographs, or return to your drawing or painting at the same time on another day. Very bright light can be filtered through muslin or blinds. Fascinating effects can be achieved by allowing light to shine through slatted blinds so that bands of light and shadow drape themselves across the undulations of the form.

The advantage of artificial light is that it is predictable and controllable. It can be brightened or dimmed, directed on to the subject or bounced off an adjacent surface. An adjustable desk light or spotlight can be used to create a dramatic directional light.

Light from above gives a fairly even distribution of highlight and shadow and the details of the figure are easy to read.

Light from the front flattens the form and provides little contrast of light and shadow, but the facial features are clearly visible.

Light coming in from the left throws the right side of the figure into shadow. Side light can be atmospheric and informative.

Light coming from behind emphasizes the silhouette. The figure drawn and painted contre jour *has an ambiguous quality.*

SETTING UP A *CONTRE JOUR* POSE

Position the model so that the main light source is behind her, but make sure there is enough overall light to illuminate the front of the figure as well. The silhouette is an important element in this composition, so find a pose that creates an interesting shape on the page, and choose dark, flowing garments that emphasize the silhouette.

SEATED WOMAN, *CONTRE JOUR*

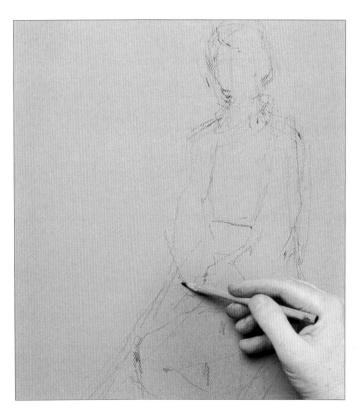

Materials and Equipment

- SHEET OF TINTED PASTEL PAPER
- CHARCOAL PENCIL
- PASTEL PENCILS: BLACK, BLUE, CRIMSON, YELLOW
- HARD PASTELS: WHITE, VENETIAN RED, GREY, BLACK, CYCLAMEN, FLESH TINT, RAW SIENNA, NAPLES YELLOW, SCARLET, VANDYKE BROWN, GOLD, BRIGHT PINK, RAW UMBER

1

Using a charcoal pencil, block in the main outlines of the figure. Check proportions and angles with your pencil. Use the verticals and horizontals in the background to locate the components of the figure accurately.

2

Organize the figure on the paper so that it makes a satisfying composition. Here, the model is placed to one side to create an asymmetric design. The predominant vertical of the perched figure is counterpointed by the diagonal of the outstretched leg. Develop the drawing, looking for the way the different parts relate to each other and to the stool. Check these relationships by extending lines from one part of the drawing to another. Consider the way the figure is balanced and visualise the body under the clothing.

3

Once the figure is broadly set out, you can begin to develop the facial details. Add a dark tone in the eye sockets, alongside the nose, on the upper lip and under the lower lip. It is useful to have a recognisable face at this stage, but don't take it too far or it will cease to be consistent with the rest of the drawing.

4

Using a pastel stick, scumble white over the screened window area. Use the stick to cut back into the silhouette, crisping up the outline. Block in the brick wall in Venetian red. Add touches of grey and black to the coat and to the model's hair. Because the support is a good mid-tone, the image feels more resolved than it would if you were working on white.

5

Scumble more white over the window area – the broken colour creates the luminosity you need for the light source. Hatch in the black of the coat, apply a glaze of Venetian red to warm the face, and add the cyclamen of the model's pullover. Start to develop the skin tones using flesh tint and raw sienna.

6

Apply a glaze of Naples yellow to the hands and then refine the shapes with the black pastel pencil and a little Venetian red. Apply black around the hands so that you are using the colour of the coat to define their outline – drawing the negative shapes is often more accurate than drawing the positive, and gives a more subtle result.

7

Stand back and study the picture from a distance, comparing the drawing with the subject. Block in the lower part of the model's flowing garments – sketching the position of the legs underneath will help you to produce a more logical drawing. Add touches of grey and scarlet to the jumper.

8

Don't focus on one part of the drawing, but try to keep the figure and the background progressing together to produce a more coherent, harmonious result. Add more scumbled white to the background and then develop the face with pastel pencils, using blue for the eyes and crimson for the lips. Pastel pencils are useful for detail, because they can be sharpened to a fine drawing point.

9

At this stage the colours are a little vibrant, so apply darker tones to create a more muted effect. Apply Vandyke brown over the brick wall and use the same colour on the face, hands and jumper. Sketch the stool with a yellow pastel pencil – it is important to the logic of the picture to describe how the model is supported.

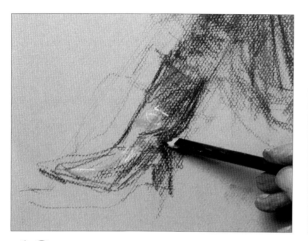

10

Add white and grey for the highlights on the shiny surface of the leather boots. Then apply the darkest tones, using the black pastel pencil. These touches of light and dark give just the right amount of detail.

11

The floor is quite light in tone compared to the rest of the picture. Use a pale colour like Naples yellow to block in the floor, taking this light tone around the stool, so that it is drawn in negative. The colour of the paper stands for the local colour of the stool.

12

Add a few tiny touches of brighter colour to show where the light catches the edge of the figure – a touch of gold in the hair, a sliver of bright pink on the collar. Hatch a little raw umber on the floor at the base of the wall, which is darker because it is not fully illuminated. The completed figure is suggested rather than accurately described. It is these hints and suggestions, the concealing and revealing of forms, that make *contre jour* such an appealing lighting effect.

DRAWING GROUPS OF PEOPLE

Drawing from a model posing in mid-movement is one thing, drawing people moving about amidst the hustle and bustle of a public place – a market, a restaurant or a station, perhaps – is quite another. But if you are to use your figure drawing skills to produce scenes from everyday life, you need to collect 'live' reference material. Get into the habit of using a sketchbook and take every opportunity to make drawings of people going about their business. You will find that your drawing skills will improve immeasurably, and you will build up a source of fascinating material on which to base drawings and paintings. Use your camera to provide back-up information – photographs are useful reference for back-grounds, colour and detail, but it is the images that you have actually drawn that remain fixed in your memory.

Market Scene, Portugal
Pencil and watercolour
40 x 32cm (16 x 12in)

SKETCHING A CROWD SCENE

In this rapid sketch, the artist has managed to encapsulate the stance and character of the main figures in just a few lines, giving them individuality even though they are not drawn in any detail. The busy market atmosphere is suggested with just a few scene-setting objects such as fruit and vegetable boxes and scales. Areas of tone denote cast shadows.

A small sketchbook is one of the artist's most useful possessions. Keep one in your pocket and work in it when you are waiting for a train, sitting in a bar or visiting a market. In locations such as these, you will often find unusual characters and interesting poses.

In a busy place like a market, people are constantly moving about, so you must look intently and try to capture the scene as quickly and economically as possible. Ignore details and observe the principal thrusts of the figures – the angles of the torso, head and limbs. At first your sketches will be rudimentary, but with practice you will get better at selecting the significant features, and your visual memory will improve, so that you can complete the sketch when the person has moved on.

When you are more confident, you can start to place people in a setting. If a person is weighing out vegetables, show the scales, the stall and some of the background. Add a few clues to the perspective, so that you have a stage

on which to put your characters. If you can sit somewhere comfortable – in a bar or café, perhaps – you can work in a large sketchbook. The format allows you to make a series of studies without constantly turning the page.

For drawing, use simple, portable materials such as a pencil, a fountain pen, a biro or a fibre-tipped pen. A few coloured pencils are useful for dashing

Here, two unrelated sketches have been placed side by side on the same page. Details such as benches, parasols, plants and shadows have been dashed in at great speed, but they tell the story very effectively.

in scribbled colour – even a few clues will help you to recall the colours in the scene. You can also annotate the sketch. Practising artists' sketchbooks are full of colour notations that are meaningful only to them.

Light is an important element of any drawing or painting, so, if you have time, make a quick thumbnail study of the distribution of light and shadow across the scene. Half-close your eyes and hatch in the areas of dark tone, paying special attention to any shadows that might be important in a composition. Make a note of the position of the sun, the time of day and the weather conditions if relevant. You will find this information helpful if you develop the sketch into a more resolved drawing or painting. You could also use a camera to take a few overall reference shots of the scene.

When you want to progress to a more detailed drawing of a scene, you can transfer your sketch to another support by using a grid of squares or rectangles. Draw the grid directly on to the sketch or draw it on a sheet of acetate and lay that over the sketch. Now draw a grid on the support to which the image is to be transferred. It must be the same shape as the original and be divided into the same number of squares. If you want the new drawing to be larger, make the squares bigger than those in the original. Then copy the drawing, square by square.

This is one of many drawings that Albany Wiseman made at the market in Lagos in Portugal. He was staying nearby and returned several times to draw. Using both pages of a landscape format sketchbook gave him a broad working area.

USING REFERENCE MATERIAL

This project is based on sketches made on location in Portugal together with a colour photograph taken at the same time. Around the main sketch the artist has made additional studies of figures and background details. He has drawn a grid of nine rectangles over the sketch, so that he can transfer it accurately to the support used for the project.

MARKET SCENE, PORTUGAL

Materials and Equipment

• 300GSM (140LB) HOT PRESSED WATERCOLOUR PAPER
• PENCILS: 4B AND 6B
• WATERCOLOURS: CERULEAN BLUE, VENETIAN RED, RAW SIENNA, FRENCH ULTRAMARINE, ALIZARIN CRIMSON, CADMIUM YELLOW
• SQUIRREL WASH BRUSH

1

Draw a grid of rectangles over the sketch and then draw a similar grid on the paper. Remember that, to avoid distortion, the picture area must have the same proportions as the original sketch. Using a 4B pencil, copy the sketch rectangle by rectangle. Work in a logical way from the foreground to the background or from the centre to the edges. This will make it easier to assess how the image is working as a composition. Work carefully but freely, so that the final drawing captures the energy of the original.

2

Once you've got the main features down, transfer details by eye using the original sketch, the photograph and your memory. Remember that you don't have to follow the original sketch slavishly. You can make additions and other adjustments if these will produce a better picture. Use your imagination or take elements from another sketch or photograph. At this stage, important components of the composition have been established – the bending figure on the left and the standing figure on the right create a broad triangle with its apex in the striped parasol near the top of the image.

3

Start to suggest the figures in the background, ensuring that they diminish in size as they move away from the foreground. Crowd scenes are potentially confusing, so it is important to have a firm compositional structure and a lucid sense of space and recession. Begin to add detail to the faces and clothing in the foreground to help bring this area into sharper focus and resolve the spatial relationships.

4

Work across the drawing, developing the key figures and the context, thinking all the time about how the image works as a composition. Sketch in the buildings in the background and suggest the diamond pattern on the pullover worn by the standing figure on the right.

5

Using the sketch and the photograph as a guide, start to hatch in areas of tone. Work lightly at first, as you can darken these areas later if necessary. The man seen in silhouette against the backlit parasol is a key focus in the composition, so start by applying tone to this figure. Don't concentrate on just one part of the drawing. The image will be more coherent if you work across the entire surface, developing it as a whole rather than section by section.

6

Use hatched tone to suggest the patterns of light and dark falling across the image. Tone can also be used to suggest the solidity of objects and figures. Shadow applied to the end of the stall-holder's crate gives it three-dimensional form, while a dark tone on his arm suggests its roundness and volume.

7

Work across the drawing, applying areas of mid tone. Stand back and assess progress so far. The drawing is broadly established, but it lacks emphasis and detail. Using a 6B pencil, start to build up the dark tones on the man beneath the parasol, in the shaded areas between figures, on dark hair and in the darkest diamonds on the standing figure's pullover.

8

Develop the faces and clothing as well as the fruit, vegetables and nuts in the foreground. Think of the composition as a series of receding planes and reserve the greatest detail for the areas in the foreground. The standing figure on the right is nearest to the picture plane, so put more detail into the pattern on the pullover and the creases and folds in the jeans. The bending figure on the left is further away and should be described with lighter tones and less detail.

9

The drawing is now complete, so you can begin to enliven it with transparent washes of watercolour. Watercolour adds glowing colour and also fixes the drawing. Using a squirrel wash brush, mix a pale wash of cerulean blue and lay this over the sky area.

10

Using the same cerulean blue wash, but varying the intensity, lay a cool blue tone over the areas of shade and cast shadow in the drawing. Allow to dry.

11

Mix Venetian red, cerulean blue and raw sienna to give a warm ochre tone and apply this to the sunlit areas in the drawing. Contrasting warm and cool colours is a powerful way of suggesting light and dark in an image.

12

Mix Venetian red and raw sienna to give a warm flesh tint. Apply this very loosely to the faces and hands of the foreground figures as well as to a few in the background. Use a darker tone of the same colour for the barrels of nuts in the foreground. Mix French ultramarine with alizarin crimson to paint the dark shadows on the jeans of the main figures, adding the same cool colour to the cast shadows throughout the image.

13

The clothes on the main figure on the right are painted in more detail than those on the other figures. The strong diamond pattern on the pullover, in particular, creates foreground interest. Use alizarin crimson for the crimson diamonds, applying the colour loosely.

14

Apply stripes of alizarin crimson to the parasol. This provides a visual link which leads the eye from the figure in the foreground to the parasol in the background. Complete the image by applying touches of cadmium yellow to the standing figure and the parasol, and a mix of French ultramarine and cadmium yellow to the leeks in the foreground. The image is now complete. Although it has been created in the studio from sketches and photographs made on location, it retains the energy and freshness of the original sketch.

INDEX

Accuracy, 31–37
Acrylics, liquid, 13
Anatomy, 47–49
Ardizzone, Edward, 8
Asymmetry, 66

Backlighting *see contre jour*
Balance, 50–52
Bones *see* anatomy

Cawkwell, Sarah, 21
Charcoal, 10–11, 23
Children, proportions of, 33
Cleal, John, 20
Coloured media, 12–13
Conté crayons, 12–13
Contre jour, 19, 63–69
Craft knives, 11
Crayons, 12–13
Crowd scenes, 71–79

Dancers on a Bench, 6
Degas, Edgar, 7, 9
Details, depth and, 77
Drawing boards, 11
Dry media, 12

Easels, 41
Elsie Dressing at the Dell, 18
Equilibrium, 50–51
Exercises
    accuracy and proportions, 34–37
    understanding anatomy, 50–53
    crowd scenes, 72–79
    heads, hands and feet, 58–61
    line drawing, 25–27
    capturing movement, 40–45
    tonal drawing, 28–29
    using light, 65–69
    warm-up, 15

Facial details, 51, 56, 66
Feet *see* hands and feet
Figure *see* human form
Figure drawing
    basic approaches to, 14–17
    heads, hands and feet, 55–61
    history of, 7–9
    warm-up exercises, 15–16
Fixatives, 11, 27
Furniture, as visual reference, 34

The Gleaner, 9
Graphite media, 10
Grids, 73–74
Group scenes *see* crowd scenes

Half-tones, 24
Hands and feet, 55, 57
Heads, 55–56

Human form
    anatomy of, 47–49
    attributes of, 17
    hands and feet, 55, 57
    heads, 55–56
    lighting, 63–69
    moving, 20, 39–45
    proportions of, 33
    simplifying, 40–41

Inks, 11, 13

Lidzey, John, 19
Light, 16–17, 28–29, 63–69 *see also* tone
    contre jour, 19, 63–69
    direction of, 64
    natural *versus* artificial, 64
    recording in a sketch, 73
Line drawing, 23–27
Liquid media, 13

Mannikin figures, 40–41
Market scenes, 74–79
Masai Warrior, 20
Masking tape, 36
Materials and equipment, 10–13
    accessories, 11
    acrylics, liquid, 13
    charcoal, 10–11
    coloured media, 12–13
    crayons, 12
    graphite media, 10
    inks, 11, 13
    pastels, 12
    pencils, 10, 13
    pens, 11, 13
    sketching, 73
    watercolours, liquid, 13
Models *see also* poses
    choosing a pose, 25–29
    lighting, 65
    moving, 41–45
    nude, 34–37
    resting, 35
    working with, 16–17
Movement *see* human form, moving
Muscles *see* soft tissues

'Negative' shapes, 25, 32, 36, 67
Nudes, 34–35, 36–37

Oil pastels, 12

Papers, 13
Pastels, 12, 68
Pencils
    coloured, 13
    graphite, 10
    measuring with, 32
    pastel, 12

water-soluble, 13
Pens, 11
    fibre-tipped (coloured), 13
Perspective, 31, 52, 72
    pre-Renaissance, 8
Photographs, as reference material, 71, 73, 74, 79
Pontefract, Susan, 20
Poses, 25–29
    bending, 45
    contre jour, 65–69
    showing hands and feet, 58–61
    moving, 41–45
    seated, 28–29, 36–37, 52–53, 58–61, 65–69
    standing, 25–27, 34–35, 50–51
    stretching, 44
    timed, 26
Proportions, 32, 33, 34–35

Recession *see* perspective
Rembrandt, 7, 9
Renaissance, 8–9

Seurat, Georges, 9
Sharpeners, 11
Simplification (of human form), 40–41
Skeleton *see* anatomy
Sketching, 71–73
Skulls *see* heads
Soft tissues, 49
Spines, 48, 49
Studio sticks, 12
Study of a Nude Woman, 7
Stumps *see* torchons

Tom, Watching TV, 20
Tone, 23–24, 28–29, 76
Torchons, 11
Tortillons *see* torchons

Up Over my Head, 21

Warm-up exercises, 15
Water-soluble pencils, 13
Watercolours
    liquid, 13
    washes of, 77
Wax crayons, 12
Whittlesea, Michael, 21

Young Dancer, 21

PICTURE CREDITS
The author and publishers would like to thank the following for permission to reproduce additional photographs:
Bridgeman Art Library (British Museum, London) 9, (Christie's Images) 7, (Glasgow Art Gallery and Museum) 6, (University of Hull Art Collection) 8.

Index compiled by Liz Atkinson.

HILLSBORO PUBLIC LIBRARIES
Hillsboro, OR
Member of Washington County
COOPERATIVE LIBRARY SERVICES